# TERRORIST ATTACKS

# THE BOMBING OF
# PAN AM FLIGHT 103

R. Doug Wicker

The Rosen Publishing Group, Inc.
New York

Published in 2003 by The Rosen Publishing Group, Inc.
29 East 21st Street, New York, NY 10010

**Library of Congress Cataloging-in-Publication Data**

Wicker, R. Doug.
The bombing of Pan Am Flight 103 / by R. Doug Wicker. — 1st ed.
  p. cm. — (Terrorist attacks)
Includes bibliographical references and index.
Summary: An account of the bombing of Pan Am Flight 103 over Lockerbie, Scotland, focusing on the events leading up to the act of terrorism, the impact on people involved, and the investigation of this crime.
ISBN 0-8239-3656-2 (lib. bdg.)
1. Pan Am Flight 103 Bombing Incident, 1988—Juvenile literature.
2. Terrorism—Europe—Juvenile literature. 3. Terrorism—United States—Juvenile literature. 4. Bombing investigation—Scotland—Lockerbie—Juvenile literature. [1. Pan Am Flight 103 Bombing Incident, 1988.
2. Bombing Investigation. 3. Terrorism.]
I. Title. II. Series.
HV6431 .W515 2003
363.12'465'0941483—dc21

                                                      2001007017

*Manufactured in the United States of America*

# CONTENTS

# INTRODUCTION

Colonel Muammar al Qaddafi, the leader of Libya, called it his "Line of Death." If investigators are correct, President Ronald Reagan's decision to cross that line started a chain of escalating events that would lead, thirty-three months later, to one of the worst aviation disasters in history.

Colonel Qaddafi's Line of Death extended Libya's territorial claims well beyond those recognized under international law. His intent was to exclude United States naval forces from operating inside the Gulf of Sidra. Trouble had been brewing between the United States and Libya ever since Qaddafi's rise to power in 1969, when he closed U.S. military bases in Libya and began training and financing terrorists from around the world.

To ensure the freedom of any nation to navigate international waters, in March 1986 President Reagan ordered three aircraft carrier task forces from the U.S. Navy's Sixth Fleet to cross the Line of Death in a "freedom of navigation" exercise. On March 24, 1986, Libyan air defense fired missiles at two U.S. naval aircraft.

President Ronald Reagan's decision to challenge Muammar al Qaddafi's Line of Death eventually led to the bombing of Pan Am Flight 103.

Although neither aircraft was hit, Libya had now unlawfully attacked aircraft operating in international airspace. President Reagan ordered retaliatory strikes, resulting in the destruction of the Libyan missile site and targeting radar.

Five Libyan navy ships approached to within threatening distance of the U.S. fleet and were ordered to withdraw. When the Libyan navy ignored this warning, the U.S. Navy attacked and sank two of the ships.

The skirmishes appeared to end. The Libyan military stopped its aggressions. But Colonel Qaddafi had merely gone from using his military forces to calling upon his secret, worldwide network of terrorist armies.

On April 2, 1986, a bomb planted on board TWA Flight 840 exploded, killing four Americans. Blame was never assigned, but authorities suspected Qaddafi's handiwork. Three days later, a bomb exploded in a Berlin disco. Of the 200 people injured, roughly one-third were American military service personnel. One American serviceman and a civilian were killed. Communications intercepted by German and U.S. intelligence agencies showed that Colonel Qaddafi had ordered the attack. With direct evidence in hand, President Reagan decided to send a message Colonel Qaddafi would not soon forget.

On April 15, 1986, the United States attacked several Libyan terrorist training facilities. Unfortunately, the French Embassy in Tripoli was hit inadvertently, killing seven civilians and injuring many more. Colonel Qaddafi's house was damaged. It was claimed that he was struck and injured by flying debris, and that his adopted daughter was killed. The Libyan leader disappeared for twenty-four hours. When he finally reappeared, he was uncharacteristically quiet and reserved. It was assumed that he had been successfully frightened.

But fourteen years later, Scottish prosecutors would claim that this was not the case. Colonel Qaddafi was merely planning his revenge. Terror was Qaddafi's weapon of choice, and he believed a civilian target would bring more terror than targeting the U.S. military. Terror would also supply Libya with a cloak of anonymity that a direct military confrontation would not.

Colonel Qaddafi waited as the Libyan intelligence service poked and prodded for a weakness in airline security. That weakness would surface on December 21, 1988. Colonel Muammar al Qaddafi would get his revenge by planting a bomb on Pan Am Flight 103. Two hundred fifty-nine innocent men, women, and children on board and eleven others would lose their lives when flaming remnants of the massive Boeing 747 rained down upon the small Scottish town of Lockerbie.

This dramatic image of the *Maid of the Seas* cockpit illustrates the force of the bomb used to bring down Pan Am Flight 103.

# TOO MANY SUSPECTS, TOO FEW CLUES

## CHAPTER 1

The days following the destruction of Pan Am Flight 103 were marked by wild speculations. An unfortunate by-product of any disaster is the need to place blame. Stereotypes replace reason. Bigotries and prejudices emerge. Valuable time is wasted chasing unfounded suspicions. The Lockerbie disaster would prove no different.

Because of a troubled history with the United States, suspicion was initially directed toward Iran. The list of suspects did not stop there, however. Many Arab groups were accused. Palestinians topped many people's list of suspects. So did Syrian operatives.

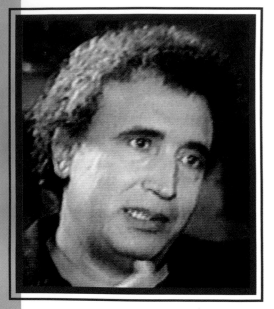 

Libyans Abdelbaset Ali Mohmed al-Megrahi *(left)* and Al Amin Khalifa Fhimah were accused of murder in the bombing of Pam Am Flight 103. Al-Megrahi was found guilty and imprisoned, while Fhimah was acquitted and freed.

So bad was the climate of accusation that Hussein Ibish of the American-Arab Anti-Discrimination Committee remarked, "Whoever is out of favor at the moment has been blamed. The whole Arab world got blamed."

## The Speculation Ends

In a joint announcement on November 14, 1991, the United States and Great Britain announced that criminal charges had been filed against two Libyan citizens. It was claimed that the suspects, Abdelbaset Ali Mohmed al-Megrahi and Al Amin Khalifa Fhimah, were both agents of the Libyan intelligence service Jamahiriya Security Organization (JSO).

Libya is a closed society. Access to its citizens, officials, and government records is tightly controlled. As such, a truly detailed and accurate depiction of the two suspects is all but impossible to obtain. What is known about them was gathered by intelligence agencies or from their activities outside Libya.

At the time of the bombing, Al Amin Khalifa Fhimah was the Luqa Airport station chief for Libyan Arab Airlines' operations on the island of Malta. Abdelbaset Ali Mohmed al-Megrahi also worked for Libyan Arab Airlines on Malta, as head of LAA's local airline security section. But were they truly airline employees, or was their presence at Luqa Airport a convenient cover for something far more sinister?

Investigators attempted to link both men to the JSO. The JSO has a long, well-documented history of organizing and financing terrorist organizations around the world. It also had direct links with the Soviet bloc. After the fall of Communism, it was revealed that in the mid 1980s Libya obtained from Czechoslovakia 1,000 tons of a newly developed, highly effective, and virtually undetectable explosive called Semtex. Documents made public later show that in March 1990, the president of Czechoslovakia declared this an amount to be "sufficient to support terrorism throughout the world for 150 years."

# TERRORISM

Certain groups and nations use terrorism to further their goals for several reasons. Terrorism is cheap, much more so than all-out war. Terrorism provides anonymity; if strict secrecy is maintained, the victimized nation may never know with absolute certainty who is behind the act. Terrorism is an equalizer—when dealing with a vastly superior military power, terrorism is the only way a group or nation can compete. Terrorism works to change the opinions of a nation's people, prompting them to question their government.

But terrorism has its drawbacks for the terrorists. If terrorists remain silent, the reasons for the attack are unknown and the terrorists' ultimate goals are never met. The victimized nation can only wonder about the motives behind the attack. If the terrorists' identities are revealed, they open themselves up to hatred from the rest of the world, isolation, economic sanctions, and revenge attacks from an angered nation's military forces. Instead of breaking the victimized nation, terrorism can actually strengthen it.

Shortly after Libya acquired this state-of-the-art explosive, Semtex began appearing in terrorist activities around the world. Groups as diverse as the Popular Front for the Liberation of Palestine-General Command (PFLP-GC) and the Irish Republican Army (IRA) received shipments. The IRA alone took possession of over two tons of Semtex from Libya.

Who better than an airline employee to find ways to get around airline security and plant an explosive device? If investigators were correct, al-Megrahi and Fhimah were perfect choices to carry out Colonel Qaddafi's plans for revenge. There was a problem, however. How would two Libyan Arab Airlines employees in Malta find a way to strike a Pan American Boeing 747 departing from another airport? Was it even possible? Sadly, it would prove all too easy.

Pan Am Flight 103 took off from London's Heathrow Airport at 6:25 PM local time and soon disappeared from the radar screens of air traffic controllers. Its wreckage was scattered over the countryside near Lockerbie, Scotland, a town of 2,500 people some 275 miles northwest of London.

Almost two weeks after Pan Am Flight 103 was blown from the sky, parts of the plane's tail were found fifteen miles away from Lockerbie.

# ON THE GROUND AND IN THE AIR OVER LOCKERBIE

## CHAPTER 2

Captain James B. MacQuarrie was fifty-five years old and lived in Kensington, New Hampshire. His flying experience included everything from propeller planes to jets. He started out in the aircraft that revolutionized commercial aviation: the 1930s-vintage twin-propeller DC-3. He advanced to the world's first commercially successful jet airliner, the Boeing 707. Later, he would fly the Boeing 720 and also the large Lockheed L-1011. He had logged 10,910 hours of flying experience.

On December 21, 1998, helming Pan Am Flight 103, Captain MacQuarrie was at the pinnacle of his career. He

James B. MacQuarrie was the pilot of Pan Am Flight 103.

commanded the largest airliner ever built, the magnificent Boeing 747. His experience in the 747 totaled 4,107 hours. MacQuarrie had the knowledge, experience, and temperament to handle any emergency. If an emergency was survivable, MacQuarrie was the man to have in the captain's seat.

MacQuarrie's right-hand man, literally, was First Officer Raymond R. Wagner. Wagner lived in Pennington, New Jersey. Three years younger than MacQuarrie, copilot Wagner's experience was in many ways even more impressive. He held certifications in the Boeing 707, 727, and 747. He had 11,855 hours of flight time—5,517 hours in the 747.

Behind MacQuarrie and Wagner sat the flight engineer. At forty-six, Jerry D. Avritt was the youngest member of the cockpit crew. He had 8,068 hours of flying experience. His 747 time totaled 487 hours. He lived in Westminster, California.

The cabin crew consisted of Chief Purser Milutin Velimirovich, an American living in Middlesex, England; Purser Mary Murphy, also of Middlesex; and eleven flight attendants, seven of whom were American citizens. Although Pan American World Airways was an American carrier, this crew was truly international.

## The Passengers

Major Charles D. McKee was in the U.S. Army. His friends jokingly called him Tiny, although he was anything but. He weighed 270 pounds but carried it well on his six-foot, five-inch frame. His current assignment was with the Defense Intelligence Agency. He was stationed in Beirut, Lebanon, and he was familiar with the Arabic language. He would be in seat 15F when the front of the aircraft ripped away.

Flora Swire was twenty-three years old. She was studying medicine in Europe, and boarded Pan Am 103 on December 21 to visit her boyfriend in New York. Her seat assignment was 39D. Her parents, Jane and Jim Swire, would later become instrumental in organizing the families of the victims and insuring that justice would one day prevail. It was through their efforts that Pan Am 103 was not allowed to fade from the public conscience.

Just before the doors to Pan Am 103 were closed, Judi Papadopoulos of North Lawrence, New York, received a call from her husband, Chris. He was returning from a business trip to Yugoslavia. He had stopped over in London for additional meetings. Judi told *Newsday* that the last words he said to her were, "I'm getting on the plane now." He then took seat 17G.

The families of the victims of the bombing of Pan Am Flight 103 banded together in a thirteen-year struggle to bring the Libyan terrorists to justice.

*Left:* Daniel and Susan Cohen lost their daughter, Theodora, on Flight 103.

*Right:* Rosemary Wolfe's daughter, Miriam Luby, was killed in the bombing.

*Left:* Sisters Bettina Solomon *(left)* and Vivien Friedman display a picture of their brother, Marc Tager, who was killed on Flight 103.

Mark Tobin, a Fordham University student, had been studying in England. He was twenty-one years old. Whenever he was on break, he worked at the Marriott Hotel in Uniondale, New York. On December 21, he was returning to the job to pay for a room for his sister and brother-in-law when they visited over the holidays. He spent his last moments in seat 32G.

Jocelyn Reina had been a flight attendant with Pan Am for just eleven months when she boarded Flight 103. She was originally from Los Angeles, California, but at the time lived in Isleworth, England. Before starting her career with Pan Am she had studied drama. She had acted in commercials, including one for Disneyland. She was twenty-six years old.

Khalid Nazir Jaafar was a twenty-year-old student. He had been in West Germany visiting friends. He was assigned to seat 53K. His was the only Arabic name on the passenger list. Later, when racism and paranoia began to surface, his family would pay dearly.

In the days immediately following the bombing, suspicion would fall on the young man. Reporters would camp outside the Jaafar family's home in Dearborn, Michigan. Classmates would target his nine-year-old sister and ten-year-old brother for torment. The *Washington Times* quoted sources "close to the family" that the Jaafars believed Syrians may have tricked Khalid into carrying the bomb. The *Washington Times* never called the Jaafar family to verify the story before running it. Some British newspapers and the television network CNN reported that a Libyan terrorist had presented the radio that housed the bomb as a gift to Khalid. In the end, the FBI would discount all these accusations. However, the emotional damage that these reports caused the family had already been done.

Syracuse University in New York State was particularly hard-hit by the events of December 21. Thirty-five Syracuse University students were on board Pan Am Flight 103. They included twin brothers from Mendham, New Jersey, named Jason and Eric Coker. They were assigned to seats 43A and B. Aspiring actress Theodora Cohen was twenty. She occupied seat 21H. Alexander Lowenstein, in seat 20D, was majoring in marketing. He planned on obtaining a degree in clinical psychology. Richard P. Monetti of Cherry Hill, New Jersey, wanted to be a journalist. Instead, sitting in seat 20E, he would be a casualty of one of the biggest news stories of the 1980s. Most of the Syracuse University victims were between nineteen and twenty-one years of age.

Gabriel Della-Ripa worked for Pan Am, but on this day he was a passenger, not a member of the crew. He was returning from a vacation in Italy, where he had visited his mother. He would leave behind a wife and two daughters. His seat, 2B, placed him in the first part of the aircraft to break away, plunging 31,000 feet.

Flowers bloom at Syracuse University's Wall of Remembrance, a memorial to the thirty-five Syracuse students killed in the bombing of Flight 103.

The crash of Pan Am Flight 103 turned this quiet neighborhood in Lockerbie into a scene of destruction and carnage.

These are just some of the passengers and crew who occupied Pan Am Flight 103. We know their names, their birth dates, even their seat assignments. We cannot know the terror they felt in their last moments of life. They also would not be the only ones to die that day.

## On the Ground

In Lockerbie, Scotland, there was a small residential area known as Sherwood Crescent. A Boeing 747 on a transatlantic flight carries an enormous amount of fuel in its wings. Sherwood Crescent would be ground zero for those massive wings.

One of the houses on the ground in Lockerbie belonged to an elderly couple, Dora and Maurice Henry. The Somerville family also owned a home in Sherwood Crescent. In that home were John and Rosalind and their two children, thirteen-year-old Paul and ten-year-old Lynsey.

Steven Flanagan was walking to his home in Sherwood Crescent when Pan Am Flight 103 fell to Earth. He would be half a block away when Sherwood Crescent exploded. He would be the only surviving member of his family—a witness to the devastation that would take the life of his father, Thomas; his mother, Kathleen; and his sister, Joanne. More names were to be added to the Lockerbie casualty list.

At precisely 6:25 PM local time on December 21, 1988, the nose of Pan Am Flight 103 lifted off the runway. None of the people on board could know they had just thirty-eight minutes to live.

Parts of Pan Am Flight 103 slammed into a row of houses and a gasoline station in Lockerbie, igniting a fireball that rose 300 feet into the sky.

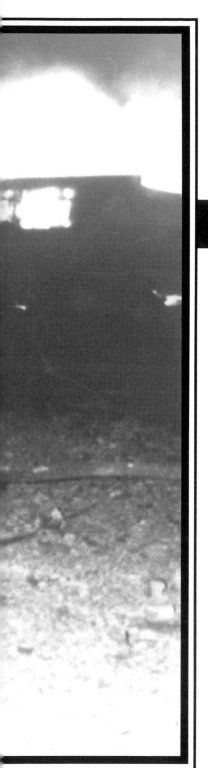

# AN UNESCORTED BAG, AN UNDETECTED BOMB

## CHAPTER 3

The destruction of Pan Am Flight 103 didn't start with the victims. It didn't begin in England on December 21, 1988. The destruction of Pan Am 103 began months earlier in far-away places. The intricate web of evidence spans continents. The list of suspects fills pages.

In October 1988, the West German Federal Police had raided several homes and businesses in Neuss, a city near Düsseldorf. Eighteen members of PFLP-GC were arrested. Four bombs were confiscated in the raids. The bombs were built to detonate with changes in barometric pressure. These are sometimes called aircraft or altitude bombs because when an aircraft gains altitude the barometric pressure around the aircraft decreases. The explosive used was Semtex. The bombs were hidden in Toshiba radio cassette players. The maker of those bombs, a Jordanian named Marwan Khreesat, claimed that he had made a total of five. The fifth was supposedly never found, but some believe it was— when Pan Am Flight 103 exploded over Lockerbie.

## The Bomb

Prosecutors would present a detailed account of the activities of Abdelbaset Ali Mohmed al-Megrahi and Al Amin Khalifa Fhimah in the weeks leading up to the bombing of Pan Am 103. Some of this account remains speculation. Some is based upon the words of the defendants themselves, particularly from Fhimah's diary. Some comes from eyewitnesses. Some of the preparations for the bombing remain a mystery to this day.

Only the conspirators know for certain when the bomb was manufactured and by whom. What is known is its construction. Investigators would piece together in surprising detail precisely how it was made. It was a time bomb. It contained approximately 450 grams (one pound) of the high-energy explosive Semtex, probably part of the vast supply acquired by Libya from Czechoslovakia in the mid 1980s. The timer was an MST-13 made by MEBO Electronics of Zurich, Switzerland. MEBO had sold a supply of MST-13 timers to the Libyan government in 1985. One of the Libyan government's representatives for the MST-13 deal was al-Megrahi.

Investigators recovered these fragments of the suitcase that held the bomb that brought down Flight 103. The fragments were used as evidence in the case against the Libyan terrorists.

The bomb was hidden in a Toshiba radio cassette player. Ironically, the model name was the Toshiba BomBeat. The Toshiba was repacked in its original box and then placed inside a brown, hard-shelled Samsonite suitcase. The suitcase was then packed with clothing and an umbrella. The clothing and the umbrella were traced to a store on the island of Malta.

Mary's House is a clothing store in Sliema, Malta. According to shopkeeper Tony Gauci, about two weeks before Christmas 1988, a Libyan man entered Mary's House. The Libyan spoke to Mr. Gauci in a mix of Arabic, English, and Maltese. The customer purchased clothing identical to that packed in the bomb-laden suitcase. The man also purchased an umbrella. Weeks later, fragments from an identical umbrella would be found on the Scottish countryside.

Police questioned Mr. Gauci nine months after the bombing of Pan Am 103. It would take that long to trace the clothing and umbrella back to his store. Mr. Gauci did not get all of his facts straight. Records show that the purchase was made closer to four weeks before Christmas rather than two.

Mr. Gauci remembered other things, however, with detailed accuracy. He remembered precisely the specific items purchased. He recalled the appearance of the customer well enough to identify him from photographs. But why would Mr. Gauci remember a purchase made ten months earlier in such detail? What triggered his recollection, he says, was the odd behavior of the customer. The customer purchased clothing randomly, with apparently no regard to the sizes or prices. The purchaser, according to Mr. Gauci, was al-Megrahi.

The primary mystery remains. How does a man on Malta place a suitcase containing a bomb onto an aircraft in London? He would need help. He would need the expertise of someone in the airline industry. He would need someone with access to the innermost workings of the tight security methods used by airlines to transfer luggage. He would need the help of Al Amin Khalifa Fhimah.

## Getting the Bomb on the Plane

Police obtained Fhimah's diary in a search of his business office in 1991. The diary was damning. One entry stated that on December 15, 1988, Fhimah had gone to his job at Malta's Luqa Airport, where he was the station chief for Libyan Arab Airlines. In violation of security procedures, he picked up some Air Malta baggage tags for "Abdulbaset/Abdussalam," a clear reference to Abdelbaset Ali Mohmed al-Megrahi. This entry also implied that al-Megrahi used an alias. Three days later, on December 18, Fhimah flew to Tripoli, Libya. He returned on December 20. On that same flight was al-Megrahi.

Prosecutors contend that Fhimah flew back from Tripoli with al-Megrahi for a very specific reason. It was alleged that al-Megrahi was returning to Malta with the makings of the bomb. His luggage was subject to a search by Maltese customs officials upon his arrival. Fhimah's luggage, however, was a different matter.

As station chief, Fhimah was well known to the customs officials at Luqa Airport. It was unlikely that customs would bother to check his luggage. Placing the bomb parts in Fhimah's luggage would considerably reduce the possibility that they would be discovered. Thus, the bomb parts entered the island of Malta undetected.

The bomb parts were reassembled and placed inside the Toshiba BomBeat. Al-Megrahi set the MST-13 timer to detonate the Semtex at approximately 7:00 PM London time. He placed the Toshiba into the Samsonite case packed with the clothing and umbrella purchased from Mary's House in November. He then took one of the Air Malta luggage tags obtained by Fhimah, marked the routing on it, and attached it to the suitcase. The tag called for the suitcase to travel from Malta to Frankfurt, Germany, aboard Air Malta Flight KM180. It would then be transferred to Pan Am Flight 103A, a Boeing 727 to London, and continue on board New York–bound Pan Am Flight 103, the ill-fated Boeing 747.

The suitcase was brought to Luqa Airport. Investigators would contend that somehow security was bypassed and the suitcase was loaded onto Air Malta flight KM180. This was never adequately proven to the satisfaction of the Scottish judges who would later hear the case. There is no record of an unaccompanied bag having been loaded onto KM180. There is, however, a computer record that a bag was transferred from KM180 to Pan Am 103A, even though there

Fhimah used his position as station chief for Libyan Arab Airlines at Malta's Luqa Airport, seen here, to route the bomb through the baggage systems of three airports.

were no connecting passengers. Although questions remain as to precisely how the Samsonite found its way aboard Pan Am 103 in Heathrow, this is considered the most likely scenario.

One thing is certain, however. On December 21, just one day after returning to Malta from Tripoli, Fhimah boarded another flight back to Tripoli. Also booked on that flight was Ahmed Khalifa Abdusamad. Abdusamad's passport was Libyan, issued to him by the Libyan government. That passport was a fake. Abdusamad was al-Megrahi. Al-Megrahi had at least three other fake Libyan passports, and he used a total of nine aliases.

## Preparing for Takeoff

Hidden inside a cassette player within a suitcase, the bomb was slowly winding its way through the baggage systems of three airports. It is thought that Air Malta KM180 carried the Samsonite case to Frankfurt. There is no doubt, however, that Pan Am 103A carried the bomb to Heathrow Airport in London.

Passengers for Pan Am 103 to New York came from many locations. Forty-nine were connecting from Pan Am 103A. Some were connecting from other airlines. Still others arrived at the airport via ground transportation—cars, taxis, buses, even trains. At Gate 14, the boarding call for Flight 103 was made. Sixteen crew members waited aboard the Boeing 747 for the 244 ticketed passengers to settle in. The passengers boarded—all the passengers except one. That passenger, a U.S. citizen, had checked in himself and two bags at Heathrow Airport.

The bags were loaded into the cargo hold of Pan Am 103. When the passenger failed to show up at the gate, airline officials debated about what to do. Searching for and removing the passenger's bags would delay the flight, which was already late. Eventually, the airline officials decided to allow the departure to continue with the baggage still on the aircraft. The aircraft pushed back from the gate at 6:04 PM London time. Those on Pan Am Flight 103 had just under an hour to live.

Boeing introduced the 747 in 1969. A fully-loaded aircraft contains some 350,000 pounds of fuel. Pam Am Flight 103 took off with 200,000 pounds of fuel.

Was the missing passenger somehow associated with the bomb? Investigators would later determine that he had been drinking at the airport bar and had failed to hear the boarding call. Though he probably didn't feel this way when he realized the Boeing 747 departed without him, he was for a time the luckiest man alive. By missing the flight, he had saved his life.

A rescue worker walks among the wreckage of Pan Am Flight 103.

# The Death of the Maid of the Seas

## CHAPTER

December 21, 1988. Christmas was just four days away. Passengers wanted desperately to get home, to spend the holidays with friends and relatives. Pan Am 103 was running about thirty minutes late. The aircraft pushed away from the gate at 6:04 PM local time in London. The engines were started. The plane taxied to Runway 27 Right for departure. The crew completed their pre-flight checklist. Congestion on the ground made the aircraft even later. It took twenty minutes to get into takeoff position. Everything appeared normal.

The Boeing's digital flight data recorder (DFDR) and cockpit voice recorder (CVR) are known as black boxes, although they are painted bright orange to help in locating them after an accident. The DFDR, CVR, air traffic voice and radar recordings, seismographs, and eyewitness accounts reveal in detail the final minutes of Pan Am 103.

The nose wheel of the giant aircraft lifted off the pavement at 6:25 PM , carrying 259 passengers and crew members into the sky. The aircraft turned northward, heading 350°, and climbed to 6,000 feet. Passing safely beneath an aircraft in a holding pattern, the aircraft continued its climb to 12,000 feet, then to 31,000 feet. The fight attendants began serving drinks and distributing menus. Passengers reclined their seats to get comfortable. Some started reading. Others began drifting off to sleep. None had any reason to believe that anything was amiss.

The Boeing 747 leveled off at 31,000 feet as it approached the Pole Hill VOR, a VHF omni-directional radio beacon that is used for navigation. Copilot Ray Wagner dialed his radio to frequency 123.95 and called Shanwick Oceanic Area Control. Alan Topp was the air traffic controller who answered Wagner's call. The time was 6:58 PM. The MST-13 timer continued its deadly countdown.

At 7:02 PM Alan Topp began transmitting the long set of instructions that Wagner and pilot James MacQuarrie were to follow on crossing the North Atlantic. Topp watched his radar display as he issued the clearance. Something was wrong. Pan Am 103's transponder winked off. The primary radar target split into four separate targets. On the next sweep of the radar antenna, the four targets became many more. The number of radar returns multiplied with each successive sweep, until they slowly faded from view.

## The Explosion

The MST-13 timer completed its task. The bomb detonated at 7:02 PM. It would be the last sound recorded on the CVR. Electrical power to the black boxes failed.

Inside the cabin, the passengers and crew experienced an explosive decompression. Hurricane-force winds sucked toward the hole in the plane. Air rushed out of the two-foot gap at speeds of hundreds of miles per hour, peeling the plane's thin aluminum skin back like a shotgun blast ripping through a soda can. Outside, the airstream through which the Boeing 747 flew snagged the aluminum walls of the aircraft and ripped them from the fuselage. Rows of seats, with passengers still strapped in, broke free and flew into the sky. Overhead bins burst open. Carry-on bags, purses, books, and beverage trays flew through the cabin.

Three seconds after the explosion, the front section of the Boeing 747 experienced structural failure. The cockpit and first-class cabin broke from the rest of the aircraft; the main cabin was completely open to the elements. By now, the air pressure in the plane had dropped well below that necessary to sustain life. Oxygen masks dropped from the ceiling panels, but most of the passengers were probably no longer conscious.

The crash of Flight 103 gouged a 155-foot-long crater in the Sherwood Crescent neighborhood of Lockerbie.

When the cockpit ripped away, the aircraft's control cables stretched, pulled, and then broke. The main body of the aircraft pitched downward. The engines went into a full throttle. The massive airplane pitched into a dive at speeds far exceeding those for which it was designed. Pieces of the airplane started breaking away. Engines went first, followed by the fuel-laden wings. The aircraft pointed toward the small town of Lockerbie.

Air traffic controller Alan Topp desperately tried to get the attention of his supervisor. The airplane had disappeared from his radar display. Copilot Wagner had not acknowledged his oceanic clearance. Repeated radio calls to Pan Am Flight 103 went unanswered.

But Topp's supervisor was on the telephone. He had just received a call from the British Geological Survey. The seismograph at the Eskdalemuir Earthquake Monitoring Centre reported a large impact at three minutes and thirty-six seconds after 7 PM. The impact measured 1.6 on the Richter scale for measuring earth tremors. Pan Am 103 had taken a mere forty-six seconds to plunge six miles.

## The View from Below

Witnesses on the ground heard a rumbling noise, like distant thunder. It grew deafeningly loud, like a jet engine running at full speed. They looked upward and saw what first appeared to be a meteor trailing flame. The object fell into the northeastern part of town. Engine number three had arrived, burying itself into a road and warning of the destruction yet to come.

Another object fell to the earth. Boomerang-shaped and much larger than the engine, it was the wings, still joined together by the center wing box. Those wings contained an estimated 200,000 pounds of fuel. Witnesses watched as it fell onto the Sherwood Crescent residential area. They were horrified when that section of Lockerbie then disappeared in a huge fireball. The wing fuel tanks exploded on impact.

Geoffrey Carpenter was at home when the explosion blew open his front door. Later at the trial, he testified, "There was a rush of air from outside. I ran out to the front garden, and . . . there was a glow in the sky and debris up to between 400 and 600 feet in the air."

Three houses vanished without a trace. Many of the people inside were incinerated so completely that their remains were never recovered. The Somervilles and the Flanagans, along with their homes, had ceased to exist. Out of the two families, only Joanne Flanagan's body was ever found. The Henrys also perished. So did Mary Lancaster and Jean Murray, two women in their eighties.

Incredible quantities of dirt and debris were thrown into the air. The crater formed by the exploding fuel measured 47 meters, or 155 feet, more than half the length of a football field. The blast displaced 1,500 tons of dirt. Debris from the explosion traveled for miles, raining down on the countryside along with baggage and bodies from Pan Am 103.

The witnesses on the ground recoiled in horror. "The fire was falling down from the sky," Jasmine Bell later told the court. "I stepped back and back and back until my back was against the wall. I couldn't go any further." Her brother reached out and pulled her into the relative safety of his home.

Outside Stuart Kirkpatrick's home, beside the front porch, landed the body of a passenger.

Twenty-one additional homes were so badly damaged that they could not be rebuilt. They would later be bulldozed. Many more homes sustained major damage but were repairable. Considering the complete devastation of the area, Lockerbie ground casualties were remarkably light. In addition to the eleven killed, only five others were hurt. Of those five, only two sustained serious injuries.

Portions of the aircraft continued to rain down on the town and surrounding areas. A 60-foot section of fuselage fell on the Rosebank Crescent area. The impact site was 600 meters (1,980 feet) from the Sherwood Crescent crater. Engines one, two, and four fell nearby.

The forward section and cockpit landed 4 kilometers (almost 2.5 miles) east of Lockerbie. The left side was crushed on impact. The right side appeared unscathed. Kevin Anderson watched it fall next to his house. He later testified, "We went over to the cockpit to see if anyone was alive. I had a torch [flashlight]. We looked inside. I could see the pilot." Mr. Anderson could clearly read the name Pan Am had given the once magnificent flying machine. It was painted along the side. It read *Maid of the Seas.*

Bodies and body parts littered the landscape. Baggage and shreds of the plane dotted the countryside. It had been two years and eight months since Colonel Muammar al Qaddafi had allegedly lost his adopted daughter in the U.S. Air Force raid over Tripoli, a raid he provoked with an act of terrorism. Now he had his revenge.

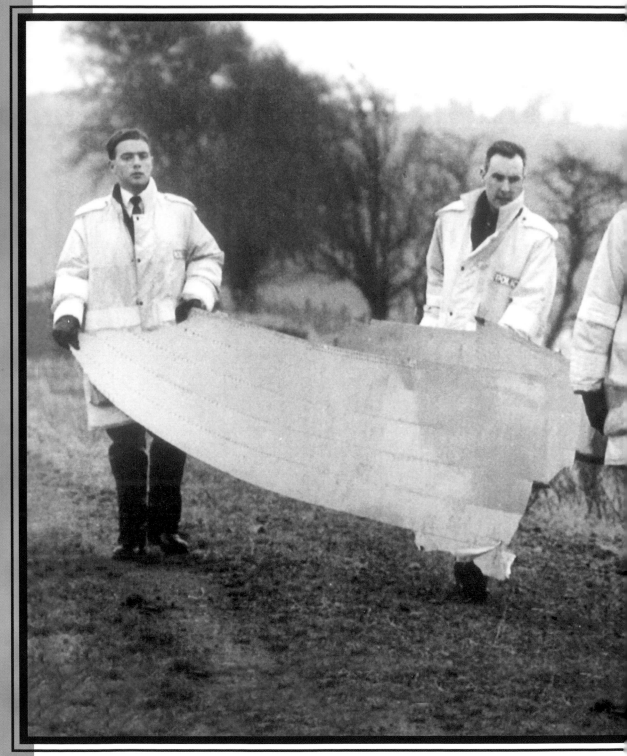

Salvagers carry a part of the plane that was found twelve miles away from Lockerbie after the explosion of Flight 103.

# A SMALL CHIP, A WHIFF OF PETN, AND A HINT OF SEMTEX

## CHAPTER 5

In response to the complete devastation of the area around Lockerbie, Scotland, twenty fire trucks were called to the scene. Royal Army and Air Force personnel responded. Police forces from surrounding areas were sent to help. Ambulances came from miles away. The Air Accident Investigation Branch (AAIB) of the British government arrived and began the gruesome task of determining what had caused the "accident." But upon seeing the wreckage, many instinctively knew this was no accident.

When an aircraft breaks apart in level flight at 31,000 feet, suspicions are raised. Pan Am 103 had done much more than just break apart. It had disintegrated. Pieces of aircraft, bodies, and luggage were scattered in two trails over a length of nearly eighty miles. Smaller debris was strewn from Lockerbie, Scotland, all the way to the east coast of England. Investigators knew the crash was probably caused by a bomb. Now they had to prove it.

In all, there would be over three million pieces from Pan Am 103 totaling 324 tons. Hundreds of people were sent into the countryside to recover every scrap they could find. The recovery operation would take many weeks and cover over 800 square miles. Eventually, through these incredible efforts, nearly 90 percent of the aircraft, its occupants, and their belongings were recovered. The most critical fragment for investigators was found three weeks after the crash, but its significance would elude them for almost two years.

## Putting the Pieces Together

The pieces from the Boeing 747 were brought to a Royal Army ammunition depot. They were laid out in their approximate relative positions. During this simple reconstruction, a hole in the fuselage was found outside the forward cargo hold. On the lower left side, in front of the left wing, was a twenty-inch by twenty-inch hole. It was apparent from the way the aluminum was peeled back that the hole had blown outward from inside the cargo hold.

The aluminum showed small pits and soot consistent with exposure to gases emanating from an explosion. Scientists examined this soot and gathered samples from the pits. In that soot were microscopic traces of two chemicals: PETN and RDX. PETN and RDX are components of the high-energy explosive Semtex. The examiners concluded that a bomb had caused the initial hole. Explosive decompression and aerodynamic stresses completed the job of destroying the aircraft.

Investigators found pieces from two suitcases near the hole. They were embedded in other sections of the aircraft's structure. These pieces were heavily pitted and covered in soot. They had to have been very near the bomb. With the discovery of the bomb's location—the forward cargo hold—investigators now concentrated on locating and piecing together the forward baggage container and anything that had been located inside.

The contents of the baggage container were gathered together and studied by investigators. Pieces showing the most damage, pitting, and soot must have been closest to the initial explosion. Slowly and meticulously, investigators waded through the mountain of fragments. Eventually, they narrowed their search for the bomb's container to two pieces of luggage. One was of metal construction. The other was made of fiberglass.

The fragments from these two containers were pieced together. On February 16, 1989, nearly two months after the bombing, this task was finally completed. It was discovered that the fiberglass suitcase had been damaged from the outside, which meant it was not the container holding the bomb. The bomb had been in the metal suitcase. That suitcase was a brown Samsonite.

Next came a detailed search among the pile of debris to find what else had been in the Samsonite. Fragments of burnt clothing were found. So were tiny pieces of an umbrella. Then came a huge discovery: a small portion of an electronic circuit board. The circuit board was traced to the type used in the Toshiba BomBeat radio cassette player. Investigators immediately tied this evidence to the arrests in Germany the previous October of bomb maker Marwan Khreesat and members of the Popular Front for the Liberation of Palestine-General Command. Suspicions turned toward Syria and Iran. Accusations began flying.

## The Investigation Continues

But this would all change. First, the particular Toshiba BomBeat model used was not quite the same as that used by Marwan Khreesat. Eighty percent of the examples produced of this model had been shipped to Libya. But something else turned the investigators' suspicions away from Syria and Iran.

Engineers reconstructed the remains of Flight 103 as part of the investigation into the bombing.

Buried in the 11,000 pieces of fabric found by searchers was the neck portion from a baby's blue and white jumpsuit. Embedded in that cloth were scraps of the Toshiba BomBeat and fragments from the Toshiba's owner's manual. Attached to the jumpsuit neck was a label. It was covered with Semtex residue. The label stated that the product was "Made in Malta" for the Malta Trading Company. Then came the find that cracked the case and pointed to the perpetrators of the crime.

Thomas Gilchrist was one of the police officers who searched the Kielder Forest in Northumberland after the crash. Kielder Forest is nearly 100 miles east of Lockerbie. On January 13, 1989, just three weeks after the crash, Gilchrist had found a portion of a gray shirt. Four days after finding the fragment, he

This bomb, hidden in a Toshiba radio/cassette recorder, was confiscated in a raid on Palestinian terrorists in October 1988 in Germany. German police issued this photo to airlines in November 1988 with a warning that such a bomb could blow up an airplane.

turned it over to investigators, who logged the cloth and placed it with other debris. It would take nearly a year before scientists began to examine it. It would be almost two years before investigators would realize that it was the key to solving the case.

Buried in the gray fragment were pieces of the Toshiba radio cassette player. Also embedded in it was a small, green piece of circuit board. Investigators removed this circuit board and attempted to determine its source and function. In June 1990, the U.S. Federal Bureau of Investigations (FBI) matched the circuit board with one made by the MEBO electronics firm of Zurich, Switzerland.

Scottish investigators interviewed Edwin Bollier and Erwin Meister, the owners of MEBO, in November 1990, January 1991, and May 1991. Bollier admitted that MEBO had supplied the Libyan intelligence service with twenty MST-13 timers. Hoping to win a contract supplying the timers to the Libyan military, he traveled to Tripoli in 1985 and personally delivered the samples.

But what did the Libyan government really want with these timers? In 1988, two Libyan terrorists were arrested in the

West African nation of Senegal. In their possession were two MST-13 timers. The first connection to Libya, and Colonel Muammar al Qaddafi, had been made.

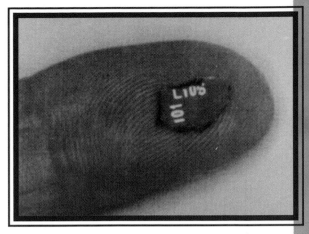

The two fragments that were crucial in tracking down the Flight 103 bombers were smaller than a fingernail.

The clothing contained in the Samsonite suitcase led the investigation to Malta. Western intelligence agents traced them to Mary's House. All Libyans living on Malta were checked. When Abdelbaset Ali Mohmed al-Megrahi, a known member of Libya's Jamahiriya Security Organization, was discovered to have worked at Luqa Airport at the time of the bombing, Western intelligence knew they had found their man. An examination of al-Megrahi's travels and professional connections led to Al Amin Khalifa Fhimah. Fhimah's diary, obtained in a police search of his offices, proved that he was the source of the Air Malta luggage tags used to route the bomb from KM180 to Pan Am 103A and finally onto Pan Am Flight 103.

On November 14, 1991, almost three years after the bombing of Pan Am 103, the U.S. and British governments jointly announced the indictment of Abdelbaset Ali Mohmed al-Megrahi and Al Amin Khalifa Fhimah. Both men now lived in Libya, under the protection of Colonel Qaddafi. Would they ever stand trial?

A van carrying Fhimah *(top)* leaves the prison facility at Camp Zeist, Netherlands, where the defendants were held in a bombproof bunker *(right)* under armed guard *(left)*.

# CAMP ZEIST: A JUDGMENT ON STATE-SPONSORED TERRORISM

**CHAPTER**

Because Colonel Qaddafi and the Libyan government refused the demands of the United States and Britain to deliver al-Megrahi and Fhimah to either country to stand trial, the United Nations (UN) took action. To pressure Qaddafi into cooperating, the United Nations directed all member nations to cancel air service with Libya and to stop the sale of weapons to the country. Any money Libya held in foreign banks was withheld, and equipment needed for oil exploration and drilling was embargoed.

Despite an embargo against his country, Libyan leader Colonel Muammar al Qaddafi refused to hand over Flight 103 bombing suspects al-Megrahi and Fhimah to the United States or Great Britain.

Denied access to desperately needed cash, oil equipment, and other necessities, Libya began to crack under the international pressure. Still Qaddafi refused to allow his men to stand trial for their alleged crimes.

United Nations secretary general Kofi Annan negotiated a solution acceptable to both sides. On August 24, 1998, the United States and Britain agreed to try the two Libyan suspects in a neutral country, but under Scottish law using a panel of three Scottish judges. Libya agreed. When al-Megrahi, Fhimah, and their lawyers left Tripoli on April 5, 1999, the UN immediately suspended the restrictions on international flights and weapons sales. Other sanctions remained in place.

The two men were taken to brand-new prison and courtroom facilities at the former U.S. airbase of Camp Zeist in the Netherlands. They would be imprisoned there until their trial, which began on May 3, 2000.

# The Trial and the Verdicts

The trial cost nearly $100 million and lasted almost nine months. The prosecutors' case was entirely circumstantial. There were no eyewitnesses to the building of the bomb, the placing of the bomb into the suitcase, the tagging of the suitcase to transfer it to Pan Am 103, or the placement of the suitcase on Air Malta Flight KM180. The prosecution had to rely on an elaborate and intricate framework of coincidences and events to make its case.

The defense team picked away at the prosecution's case. They tried to shift suspicion away from their clients by blaming the original suspects: Iran, Syria, and the Popular Front for the Liberation of Palestine-General Command. They also challenged the prosecution's charge that the defendants were members of Libya's Jamahiriya Security Organization.

Under Scottish law, as in the United States, a defendant must be found guilty "beyond a reasonable doubt." The defense team worked hard to produce that element of doubt in the three judges. For al-Megrahi and Fhimah to be found guilty, all three judges would have to be convinced that there were no other logical suspects in the case. After eighty-four days of testimony, 232 witnesses, and 2,488 pieces of evidence, verdicts were announced on January 30, 2001. Relatives of the victims lined the courtroom in anticipation.

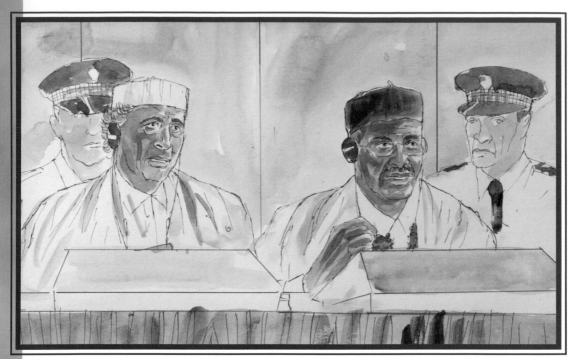
The defendants await their fate at trial in this courtroom sketch.

Abdelbaset Ali Mohmed al-Megrahi showed no emotion, staring straight ahead as judgment was passed. The court pronounced him guilty beyond any reasonable doubt. "There is nothing in the evidence which leaves us with any reasonable doubt as to the guilt of the first accused," the judges wrote.

Next came the verdict for al-Megrahi's codefendant, Al Amin Khalifa Fhimah. While the relatives of the victims would find solace from al-Megrahi's verdict, they would be sorely disappointed in Fhimah's. The court, by unanimous decision, found Fhimah not guilty.

The victims' relatives gasped in unison. Jim Swire, who had dedicated twelve years of his life to avenging the death of his daughter, Flora, collapsed. He was removed from the courtroom and taken to a local hospital.

In explaining the court's decision, the judges wrote, "Counsel for the second accused [Fhimah] argued that even if it be accepted that the second accused did obtain tags and did supply them to the first accused, it would be going too far to infer that he was necessarily aware that they were to be used for the purpose of blowing up an aircraft, bearing in mind that the Crown no longer suggest that the second accused was a member of the Libyan Intelligence Service."

After a break, the three judges reconvened the court to pronounce sentence upon al-Megrahi. Once again, the relatives of the victims were to be disappointed. Al-Megrahi would be eligible for parole and deportation to Libya just twenty years from the time he was first placed into custody. If paroled at the earliest, al-Megrahi will have served a mere twenty-seven days for each person he murdered. His conviction had been appealed and was denied in March 2002.

Upon his return, Fhimah was given a hero's reception. Libyan television broadcast his arrival live. Colonel Qaddafi greeted Fhimah with a warm embrace and declared his return a victory. No one doubts that al-Megrahi acted with the approval and help of the Libyan government. His orders had to come from high within the government, most likely from Qaddafi himself.

Peter Lowenstein, father of one of the victims, told reporters, "I am very pleased that Megrahi has been found guilty. It clearly links the Libyan government to the killing of 270 people."

Visitors pay their respects to the victims of the bombing of Pan Am Flight 103 at a memorial in Lockerbie.

Today, most UN sanctions against Libya remain in effect. They will likely continue until Colonel Qaddafi fulfills his obligations. For sanctions to be lifted, he must admit Libya's role in the bombing and compensate relatives of the victims. So far, he has done neither. In fact, he continues to deny Libyan involvement, but he has failed to provide the "proof" that he has promised will substantiate Libya's innocence.

Efforts are under way to force Libya to pay compensation. The U.S. and British governments are demanding $740 million, about $3 million per victim. UN sanctions will remain until compensation is made, but UN support for maintaining sanctions is wavering. If all UN sanctions are removed, it is doubtful that U.S. and British sanctions alone will force compensation. Additionally, Colonel Qaddafi claims the United States owes compensation to Libya for damages and loss of life incurred during the April 15, 1986, bombing of Tripoli.

Not satisfied with the compensation amounts sought by the U.S. and British governments, the Pan Am 103 and Lockerbie victims' relatives have filed a lawsuit seeking $10 billion in damages from Libya. If they win their suit, it is conceivable that Libyan assets frozen by order of the United Nations could be used to settle the claims. But it is doubtful that the claimants will ever see much in the way of compensation.

At any rate, those within the Libyan government who are responsible for the Pan Am Flight 103 bombing remain unpunished. It is hoped that justice will prevail and that these people will one day pay for their crime. As acting U.S. Deputy Attorney General Robert Mueller told reporters, "The case is not closed. The investigation will continue until any individual who played a role in this tragedy is brought to justice."

# GLOSSARY

**airstream**  The relative flow of air around an aircraft.

**air traffic control**  The ground-based system used to facilitate the safe and orderly flow of air traffic.

**Boeing 747**  The largest passenger jet aircraft currently flying. The 747 can carry up to 500 people. Used for long-range, usually transoceanic routes.

**Boeing 727**  A medium-size, three-engine passenger jet aircraft configured to carry from 163 to 189 passengers. Used for short to medium range routes.

**embargo**  A prohibition on trade with another country.

**explosive decompression**  The sudden release of pressurized cabin air from an aircraft at high altitude.

**fuselage**  The main body of an aircraft exclusive of the wings, engines, and tail section.

**Gulf of Sidra**  An inlet of the Mediterranean, along the north central coast of Libya

**Heathrow Airport**  A large international airport located outside London, England.

**indictment**  A charge against a person for a crime.

**Jamahiriya Security Organization (JSO)**  The official name for the Libyan Intelligence Service.

**PETN (pentaerythritol tetranitrate)**  A powerful puttylike explosive used in the production of Semtex and other high-energy explosives.

**Popular Front for the Liberation of Palestine-General Command (PFLP-GC)**  A terrorist organization dedicated to the creation of a Palestinian state and to the destruction of Israel.

**prosecution**  A lawyer or team of lawyers who argues a case against a defendant.

**RDX (royal demolition explosive)**  A powerfully explosive white powder used in the production of Semtex and other high-energy explosives; also called cyclonite or hexogen.

**Richter scale**  The logarithmic scale used to measure earth tremors.

**sanctions**  Pressure by a nation or nations against another nation violating international law.

**seismograph**  An instrument used to record and measure the tremors usually associated with earthquakes.

**Semtex**  A very high-energy plastic explosive developed in the former country of Czechoslovakia (now divided into the Czech Republic and Slovakia) that is very difficult to detect.

**transponder**  A device used to transmit an aircraft's identification code and altitude to air traffic control via secondary radar.

# FOR MORE INFORMATION

## Web Sites

Because of the changing nature of Internet links, the Rosen Publishing Group, Inc., has developed an online list of Web sites related to the subject of this book. This site is updated regularly. Please use this link to access the list:

http://www.rosenlinks.com/tat/bpaf/

# FOR FURTHER READING

Cohen, Susan. *Pan Am 103: The Bombing, the Betrayals, and a Bereaved Family's Search for Justice*. New York: Signet, 2001.

Deppa, Joan, with Maria Russell, Dona Hayes, and Elizabeth Lynne Flocke. *The Media and Disasters: Pan Am 103*. New York: New York University Press, 1995.

Gero, David. *Aviation Disasters: The World's Major Civil Airliner Crashes Since 1950*. Sparkford, England: Patrick Stephens Ltd., 2000.

Horton, Madelyn. *The Lockerbie Airline Crash*. San Diego, CA: Lucent Books, 1991.

Marriott, Leo, Stanley Stewart, and Michael Sharpe. *Air Disasters: Including Dialogue from the Black Box*. London: PRC Publishing Ltd., 1999.

Wallis, Rodney. *Lockerbie: The Story and the Lessons*. Westport, CT: Praeger, 2001.

# BIBLIOGRAPHY

Black, Robert. *The Lockerbie Disaster.* Vol. 3, Part 1
    Edinburgh (Scotland) Law Review, 85–95, 1999.

"Crash Blamed on Bomb 259 Aboard Jet Die; At
    Least 22 Killed on Ground." *Arizona Republic.*
    December 22, 1988.

"Devastation Permeates Lockerbie: Signs of Tragedy
    Stretch from Wreck Site to Town Hall." *Charlotte
    Observer.* December 23, 1988.

"FBI Refuses to Release Secret Lockerbie Report."
    *London Sunday Herald.* February 27, 2000.

Marriott, Leo, Stanley Stewart, and Michael Sharpe. *Air
    Disasters: Including Dialogue from the Black Box.*
    London: PRC Publishing Ltd., 1999.

McKain, Bruce, C. MacLeod, and Craig Watson. "Now
    Libya is in the Dock." *London Herald.* February 2, 2001.

Scharf, Michael P. "Lockerbie Trial Verdict." *American
    Society of International Law.* February 2001.

Sheenan, Gerard. "Timer Admission in Lockerbie Trial."
    *London Guardian.* June 21, 2000.

Yates, Chris. "The Lockerbie Disaster." *Jane's Civil
    Aerospace News.* August 1, 1999.

# INDEX

## About the Author

R. Doug Wicker is a novelist and has been an air traffic controller since 1975. He has worked in control towers and radar approach control facilities at R.A.F. Lakenheath, R.A.F. Sculthorpe, and R.A.F. Mildenhall in England; Davis-Monthan A.F.B. in Tucson, Arizona; and El Paso International Airport in El Paso, Texas.

In addition to air traffic control duties, Mr. Wicker was also charged with investigating aircraft accidents and incidents at the El Paso International Airport from 1987 until 1996. In his spare time, he writes novels dealing with aircraft sabotage.

## Photo Credits

Cover © Bryn Colton/Corbis; p. 5 © Corbis; pp. 8–9, 22, 38 © Bryn Colton/Corbis; pp. 10, 18 (middle and bottom), 27, 34–35, 47, 52 © Reuters New Media Inc./Corbis; pp. 14–15, 16, 24–25, 42–43, 48, 49 © AP/Wide World Photos; p. 18 (top) © AFP/Corbis; p. 21 © Michael Okoniewski/AP/Wide World Photos; p. 31 © Paul Almasy/Corbis; p. 33 © Bettman/Corbis; p. 50–51 (top) © Ben Curtis/AP/Wide World Photos; p. 50 (bottom left) © Dusan Vranic/AP/Wide World Photos; p. 50–51 (bottom right) © Peter Dejong/AP/Wide World Photos; p. 54 © Sian Frances/AP/Wide World Photos; p. 56 © Peter Kemp/AP/Wide World Photos.

## Editor

Christine Poolos

## Series Design and Layout

Geri Giordano